Quick & Dirty Korean for Lovers *has everything from* 작업 [pickup] *to* 침대말 [pillow talk], *from* 뽀뽀해 줘 [kiss me] *to* 날 가져! [take me] *and everything in between. Here's where you'll learn the language of love, those sweet nothings, and what to say when things go south in South Korea. Don't be cheesy, pay attention to make romance easy!*

Contents

The Straight Scoop:

Gettin' Jiggy with It

While many in the western world are more direct in approaching a prospective mate, Koreans can often be quite circumspect, so blind dates 소개팅 [so-gae-ting] are the gold standard here.

(So-gae = introduce + 'ting' from English 'meeting.')

Variations

- 소개팅 [so-gae-ting] blind date or introduction
- 미팅 [mi-ting] meeting, a group blind date
- 폰팅 [pon-ting] phone meeting
- 번개팅 [beon-gae-ting] a sudden meeting
- 헌팅 [hun-ting] hunting or chasing tail (a totally unrelated 'ting')

소개팅 해 줘.

[so-gae-ting hae juo]

Hook me up.

(on a blind date)

'cause friends hook friends up.

"Are you ready to risk it?"

Finding A Mate

6

The Straight Scoop:

부킹 [boo-king] Koreans don't routinely socialize with strangers, so the most common form of hun-ting in South Korean nightclubs is 부킹 [boo-king]. A type of forced socialization, where waiters take a girl by the wrist and pull her towards a table with a group of men. If she is interested, she stays. If the men are interested they offer a drink. ~*Time tested & effective.*

헌팅 하러 가자.

[hun-ting ha-ro ga-ja]

Let's go hunting.

Chasing Tail or what westerners might call [Regular-ting] ha ha.

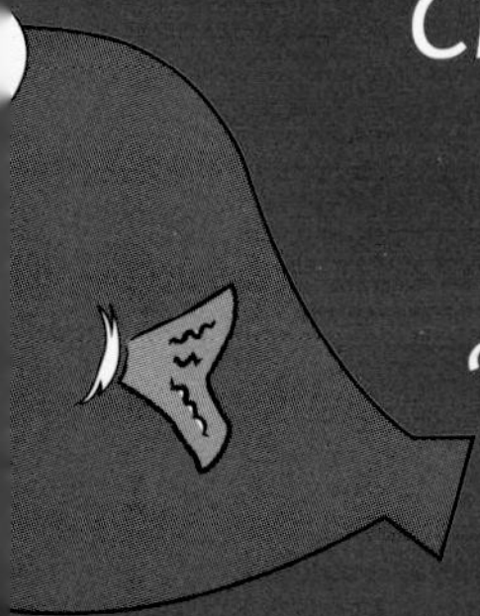

"There are plenty of fish in the sea!"

English

영어 할 수 있어요?

[yeong-eo hal su iss-eo-yo]

Can you speak English?

Pick up lines? Sorry, there aren't really any!
So just get the conversation started.

시간 좀 있어요?

[si-gan jeom iss-eo-yo]

하삼?

You got some time?

As close as it gets to Hey Honey. Warning, you may sound like a greasy pickup artist... be careful!

번호가 뭐예요?

[beon-ho-ga muo-yea-yo]

What's your number?

Can't do much without the digits!

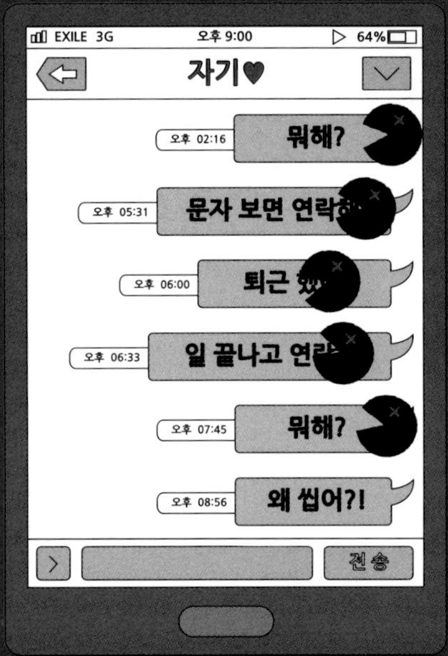

카톡해요?

[ka-tok-hae-yo]

You on KakaoTalk?

(do you KaKao)

Heard of What'sApp, well in Korea we use Kakao... It's ubiquitous, so download it and hear that telltale Obama kakao every time your lover texts you!

라면먹고 갈래?

[ra-myeon-meog-go gal-lae]

Wanna get some ramyeon?

Kinda like Netflix and chill! So let's chill at my place with some hot, spicy ramyeon.

밥 먹읍시다.

[bab meog-eub-si-da]

Let's Eat.

In a country once torn by war, food was scarce, so asking if someone has eaten is synonymous with caring.

Hooking up - Getting a date

The Straight Scoop:

Display your social status while making small talk… Dress to impress, drive a nice car, look like you matter. And have a hobby besides drinking – that will immediately impress.

술 한잔 살까?

[sul han-jan sal-gga]

Can I buy you a drink?

Drinks are delish! (And always welcome!)

달리자!

[dal-li-ja]

Let's play!

Literally, let's run, to drink is to run. Simple, yet fun! (But you have to be ready to run all night long!)

미녀

[mi-nyeo]

미남

[mi-nam]

beautiful woman

So many hotties... so little time!

beautiful man

Wow! What a hunk!

섹시

[saek-si]

Sexy

Yeah, couldn’t come up with anything better so this was borrowed from English!

개 몸짱이야!

[gae moem-jjang-i-da]

몸짱

[moem-jjang]

얼짱

[eol-jjang]

He/she's got a hot body!

A rockin' body.
A flawless face.

착하다

[chak-ha-da]

He/she's fit.

Literally "so kind." For someone kind enough to be good shape I suppose.

~좆나 섹시!

[jot-na soek-si]

존잘

[jon-jal]

존예

[jon-yea]

~so fucking sexy!

Fucking handsome!

Fucking pretty!

추남

[chu-nam]

추녀

[chu-nyeo]

A homely guy

An ugly girl

폭탄이다.

[pok-tan i-da]

He/She's a bomb.

Similar to "Falling on a grenade."
Not to be confused with "the bomb,"
which is awesome!

너 장난하냐!

[neo jang-nan-ha-ni]

You've got to be kidding!

관심없어요!

[guan-sim-eob-seo-yo]

Not interested!

Meet my hand!

내버려둬요!

[nae-beo-ryeo-dueo-yo]

Leave me alone!

For those who just don't understand NO!

사귈래요?

[sa-guil-lae-yo]

남친

[nam-chin]

여친

[yeo-chin]

Will you be mine?

Get ready to go steady!

Boyfriend
Girlfriend

사랑해!

[sa-rang-hae]

I love you!

What? Already? Yeah, I said it!

할래?

[ha-le]

Let's do it!

Is it a question or a suggestion?
Are you down? Let's get it on!

쉬었다 가자.

[sui-eoss-ta ga-ja]

MT 가자.

[MT ga-ja]

Let's go for a rest.

One goes to rest at a love motel!

Let's go to MT (Motel).

Yeah, they're on every corner.

너무 하고 싶어!

[neo-mu ha-go sip-eo]

I'm horny!

Let's pound that ground!

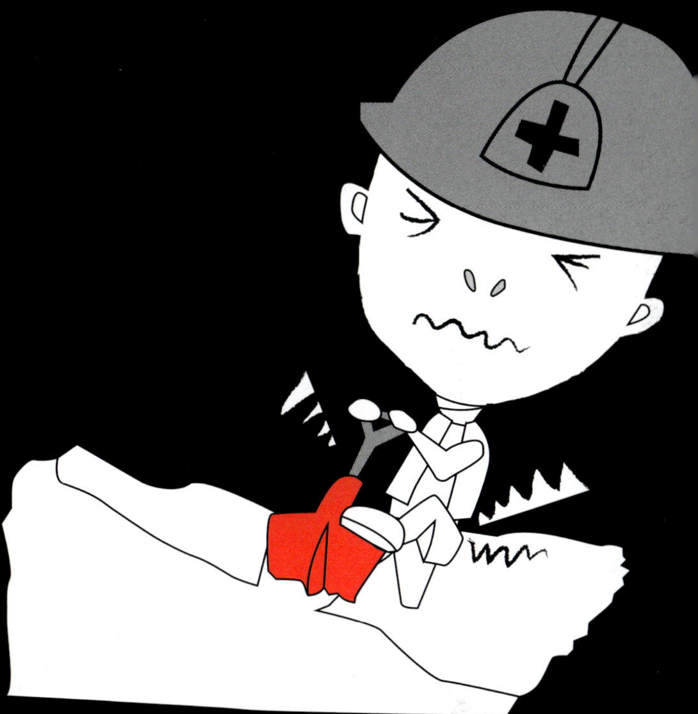

거미줄 칠 것 같아.

[geo-mi-jul chil geot gat-a]

(It's been so long)

I must have spider webs.

Only a girl would say this to her friends 'cause, well you know.

날 가져!

[nal ga-jyeo]

Take me!

A direct hit!

너 처음이야?

[neo cheo-eum-i-ya]

조심할게.

[jo-shim-hal-gae]

Is it your first time?

I'll be careful.

쌀거 같아!

[ssal-geo gat-a]

The Main Event

I'm going to cum!

T minus ten and counting...

밤의 왕이야!

[bam-ei wang-i-ya]

밤의 여왕이야!

[bam-ei yeo-wang-i-ya]

Do you have a condom?

Right here in my back pocket!
(Since like the '80s!)

나 오늘 안전한 날이야.

[na o-neul an-jeon han nal-i-ya]

떡볶이

[ddeok-bbok-i]

Safe sex - The Safety Dance

Today's my safe day.

If that's a good thing… Or a magic day!

Ddeokbboki (Days)

A popular Korean street food, Ddokbboki is spicy rice cakes, but also slang for sex during the woman's menstral cycle.

섹스

[sek-se] sex (borrowed from English)

하다

[ha-da] to do it (have sex)

자다

[ja-da] to sleep with (have sex)

떡을 치다

[ddeok-eul chi-da] hitting rice cakes (like slapping uglies)

혼전성관계

[hon-jeon seong-gwan-gae] to have premarital sex

자극하다

[ja-geug-ha-da] arouse sexual desire

성인숍

[seong-in-shop] Sex shop. To buy those awesome toys or little nightie-nothings.

자위하다

[ja-ui-ha-da] beat off or jack off

DANGER!

보지

[bo-ji] vulva, muff or pussy

자지

[ja-ji] penis or dick, also좆 [jot] cock

가슴

[ga-seum] boobs or tits

“인조이”하는 사이야.

[in-jo-I ha-neun sa-i-ya]

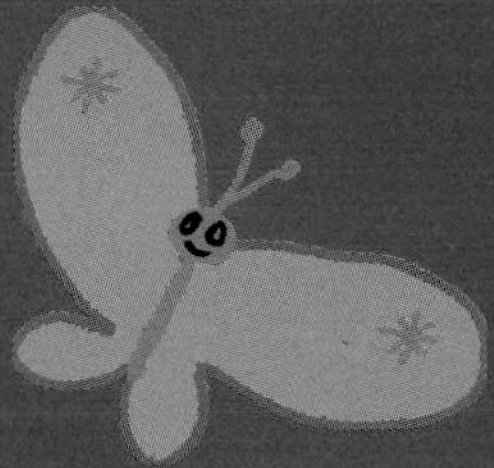

Just fooling around.

Literally, to 'Enjoy' someone's company!

진도 어디까지 나갔어?

[jin-do eo-di-gga-ji na-gass-eo]

How far did you get (with him/her)?

I don't kiss and tell... OK. Third base!

걔는 그냥 섹파야.

[gae-neun geu-nyang saek-pa-ya]

Friends with benefits.

Sex pa(rtners)... That's what friends are for.

썸타는 사이야.

[sseom-ta-neun sa-i-ya]

We got something (going on).

Something new. Something good. Something exciting. I dunno, but definitely something.

첫눈에 반했어.

[cheot-nun-ae ban-haess-eo]

Love at first sight.

As sweet as the first snow.

감동 받았어.

[gam-dong bad-ass-eo]

I’m so touched.

You’re so sweet!

난 니꺼야!

[nan ni-ggeo-ya]

I'm yours!

Now and for... well for now anyway!

오빠

[o-bba]

Big brother

Oh yeah... We went there!

자기야

[ja-gi-ya]

Baby

Literally, "oneself" as if inseparable from you. Like chocolate… mmmm chocolate.

따뜻하게 해 줘.

[dda-ddeut-ha-gae hae jueo]

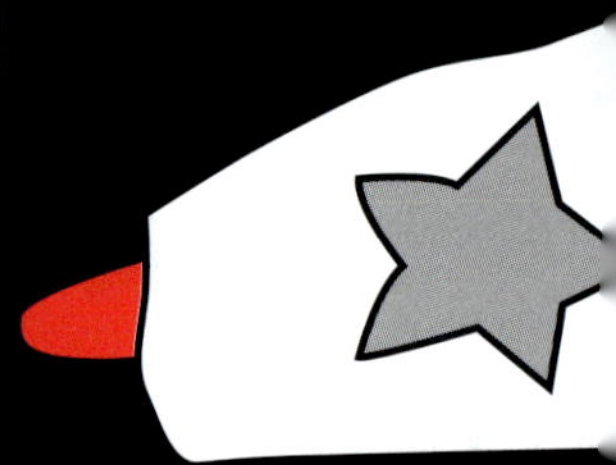

Keep me warm.

보고 싶어.

[bo-go ship-eo]

I miss you.

Soooooo much!

뽀뽀해 줘.

[bbo-bbo-hae jueo]

Kiss me.

여보

[yeo-bo]

Honey, sweetheart or my darling

Only used between a husband & wife.

나랑 결혼해줘.

[na-rang gyeol-hon-hae-jueo]

약혼

[yak-hon]

재혼

[jae-hon]

Let's get married.

Engaged

Remarried

내 말 듣고 있기는 해?

[nae mal deut-go iss-gi-neun hae]

Are you even listening to me?

변명하지 마!

[beon-myeong-ha-ji ma]

Don't make excuses!

너 질린다!

[neo jil-lin-da]

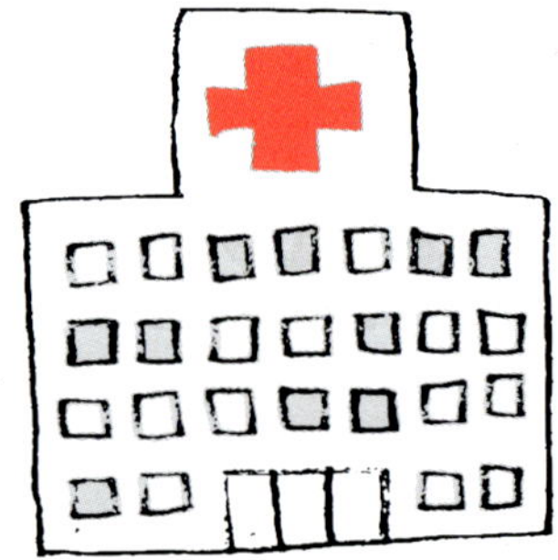

I'm so sick of you!

다른 사람 생겼어?

[da-reun sa-ram saeng-gyeoss-eo]

Is there someone else?

바람 피웠지!

[ba-ram pi-ueot-ji]

You cheated on me (didn't you)!

Busted buddy!

사과해!

[sa-gwa-hae]

Say you're sorry!

Sa-gwa can also be an apple (maybe a sad, used-up core of an apple).

꺼져!

[ggeo-jeo]

Get lost!

Ouch! That hurts!

이제 연락하지마.

[i-jae yeol-lag-ha-ji-ma]

Let's stop calling each other.

Ha! Ha!

웃기네!

[ut-gi-nae]

Don’t make me laugh!

In the most bitter way possible.

포기해.

[po-gi-hae]

Give it up.

Sometimes its better just to move on.

드디어 해방이야!

[deu-ti-yeo hae-bang-i-ya]

Finally, I'm free!

Doin' the Tom Petty (RIP)

돌싱

[dol-sing]

A Fresh Start

Single Again

Grab a spoon!